The Living Coast

The Living Coast

Richard Offen, Margaret Willes and James Parry

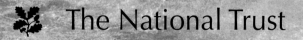

The National Trust

First published in Great Britain in 2003 by
National Trust Enterprises Ltd
36 Queen Anne's Gate
London
SW1H 9AS
www.nationaltrust.org.uk

ISBN 0 7078 0359 4

Cataloguing in Publication Data is available from
the British Library

Designed and typeset in Optima
by Peter and Alison Guy

Cover design by James Campus

Origination by Digital Imaging Ltd
Printed and bound in Hong Kong by Printing Express Ltd.

Frontispiece: Waves crashing onto rocks at Compass
Cove, Devon.
Previous page: Rocks at Holywell Bay, Cornwall.
Left: Surf on Minsmere Beach at Dunwich Heath, Suffolk.

Carrick-a-Rede
Dunseverick
Giant's Causeway
Whitepark Bay
Cushendun
Downhill

NORTHERN
IRELAND

BELFAST

ENNISKILLEN

Strangford
Lough

Murlough

Lindisfarne Castle
Farne Islands
Seahouses
Newton Haven
Embleton
Dunstanburgh
Boulmer Beach

NEWCASTLE UPON TYNE
Souter Lighthouse
Beacon Hill
Horden
Hunt Cliff, Warsett Hill
Runswick Bay
Robin Hood's Bay
Ravenscar

PENRITH

YORK

LEEDS

Formby Point

LLANDUDNO
LIVERPOOL
MANCHESTER
SHEFFIELD

STOKE-ON-TRENT

Blakeney
Point
Sheringham
Brancaster

Porthdinllaen
Llŷn Peninsula
Porthor
Braich-y-Pwll
Bardsey Island

Dinas Oleu,
Barmouth

DERBY
NOTTINGHAM

SHREWSBURY

KING'S LYNN
NORWICH

PETERBOROUGH

BIRMINGHAM

NORTHAMPTON

Dunwich Heath

Penbryn

St David's Head
Whitesands Bay
Ynys Barri
Dinas Fawr
Upper Solva
Broad Haven
Stackpole
Barafundle Bay
Rhossili
The Vile
Worms Head
Tears Point
Thurba Head

Whiteford Burrows
Llanrhidian Marsh
Three Cliffs Bay
Pennard Cliff

Gower Peninsula

CAMBRIDGE
Sutton Hoo
Orford Ness

GLOUCESTER

Northey Island
Blackwater Estuary

CARDIFF

Woody
Bay
Porlock
Bay
Brean Down

LONDON

BRISTOL
READING

Lundy
Morte
Point
Holdstone
Down
Holnicote
Estate

WELLS

SALISBURY
SOUTHAMPTON

St Margaret's-at-Cliffe
St Margaret's Bay
South Foreland
Langdon Cliffs
White Cliffs of Dover

Smallhythe Place

YEOVIL

Seven Sisters,
Cuckmere Haven
Birling Gap

West Wittering

Port Quin
The Rumps
Pentire Head
Stepper Point
Trevose Head

Sandy Mouth
Crackington Haven

Boscastle
Barras Nose
Port Gaverne
Camel Estuary

EXETER
Golden Cap

Poole Harbour
Corfe Castle
Lulworth Cove
St Aldhelm's Head

Brownsea
Island

Alum Bay
Newtown
Bonchurch Down
Tennyson Down
Compton Bay
The Needles

Saltram House

Holywell Bay
Wheal Coates
TRURO
Talland Bay
Coleton Fishacre
Dartmouth
Gammon Head
Overbecks
Scobbiscombe Farm

Seacombe
Isle of Purbeck

Studland Bay,
Ballard Point,
Old Harry Rocks

Bosigran Farm
West Penwith
St Ives
Trengwainton
Cape Cornwall
Penberth Cove
St Michael's Mount

Trelissick
St Mawes
St Anthony's Head
Durgan, Glendurgan

Helston
The
Loe Bar
The Lizard

Introduction

The sea is the lifeblood of this planet. It controls our weather, the amount of oxygen available to us to breathe and has been a rich source of food ever since man first walked the planet. Given such a powerful force, it's small wonder the coastline has had such a huge influence on the course of our history.

The coastline bears traces of man's endeavours over thousands of years and its natural resources have been at the root of our livelihood, enabling us to carry out business and even warfare with the rest of the world. Its sheer beauty has also been a source of inspiration to writers, musicians and artists alike, providing subject matter for every conceivable mood, from raging violence to peace and tranquility.

In spite of our reliance on the sea, however, we have always had an uneasy relationship with the coast. One only has to look at the countless shipwrecks that can be seen at low water around our coast, or at the reassuring sight of a lighthouse flashing its signal of impending danger, to realise that our shores have been the scene of many dramatic and life-threatening events over the centuries. Although the shoreline is an attractive place, offering countless opportunities for activities in both trade and recreation, it still needs to be treated with great respect.

Having played such an important part in our history, it was appropriate that, in 1895, the coast would be home to the first property to come to the newly formed National Trust. With the gift, by Fanny Talbot, of Dinas Oleu, a rocky hillside behind the Welsh seaside town of Barmouth, the die was cast for the Trust to play a major part in the protection of our coastal heritage. Mrs Talbot's determination that the area 'always be kept wild and never be vulgarised by the addition of asphalt paths, or cast-iron seats of the serpent design' has been respected – not just at Dinas Oleu, but in many other beautiful coastal locations as well.

Over the following hundred years, and particularly since the inauguration in 1965 of its highly successful Neptune Coastline Campaign (then known as Enterprise

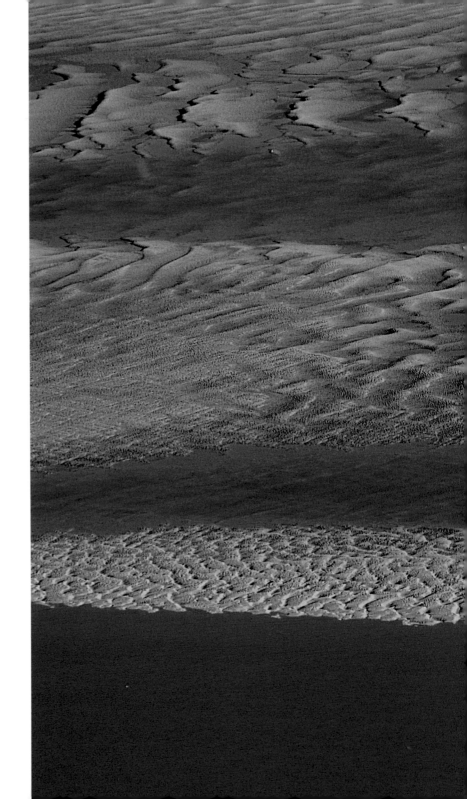

Neptune), the Trust has bought over 970 kilometres (600 miles) of spectacular coastline. This ownership amounts to about 53,000 hectares (131,000 acres) of coastal land and represents 25% of the coastline of England, Wales and Northern Ireland – no mean achievement.

In fact we often do not realise that the coastline we are enjoying is owned and protected by the Trust. Take that quintessentially British landmark, the White Cliffs of Dover, where in the past 20 years the Trust has bought over 5 miles of clifftop. Or the Lizard, Britain's most southerly mainland point, where the Trust has gradually purchased small parcels of land, with the result that the entire headland is now protected – much to the delight of the hundreds of thousands of visitors who enjoy its wild beauty every year.

It is a common assumption that, with so much coast under its protection, the Trust wants to 'preserve' our shores at all costs and protect them from any force, man-made or natural. Building walls in the sand has long been a favourite beach activity for children – it is an exciting challenge to try to keep back the incoming tide. But the sea always wins.

Some adults also like to challenge the sea by building walls of rock, concrete and steel to keep it out – or to keep the coast in. The Trust accepts that the coast is a dynamic, ever-changing landscape and that to try to pre-vent coastal change caused by natural processes is a futile gesture. The damage resulting from our attempts at pre-vention can take various forms. Some defence works are just plain ugly and would be entirely out of place on an unspoilt stretch of coast. Others cut off the supply of sand and shingle vital to maintain features such as sand bars, displacing the effects of erosion from one point to another. The coast is now very different from when the Trust was founded in 1895, and so are the ways in which it is used. Both will be different again in the future. Rather than regret the change, we should celebrate the wildness and lack of human impact on most Trust-owned coast and enjoy it for the dynamic and free thing it is.

This book sets out to reflect that 'living' coastline in all its guises. It is not intended to be a historical survey or a comprehensive gazetteer of the Trust's coastal properties, but rather a visual celebration of some of the fascinating and wonderful seaside places cared for by the Trust. There are many books that highlight the beauty of our coastal landscape; this one focuses particularly on the living creatures that make the coast their home, and as

Previous page:
The ruins of Dunstanburgh Castle on the Northumberland coast. Sand bars in Mawddach Estuary near Barmouth, Gwynedd.

Opposite top:
A view of the Golden Cap Estate, Dorset.

Opposite bottom:
Rock samphire growing on a rock face in Talland Bay, Cornwall.

Above:
A fulmar on the rocks at the Giant's Causeway, County Antrim.

Next page:
Opposite, left:
Wild flowers on Hunt Cliff and Warsett Hill in Yorkshire.

Opposite:
Gorse-covered cliff above St David's Head, Dyfed.

Above:
National Trust warden Joe Oliver walks his dog along the coast at Bosigran, Cornwall.

Right:
Two shags on the Farne Islands on the Northumberland coast.

such do so much to give coastal habitats their distinct personality. Not only the rocks, soil and sand that are the building blocks of our coast, then, but also the people, plants and animals that dwell there.

Behind every pristine-looking piece of National Trust coastline is a team of staff and volunteers that works tirelessly to ensure that the natural beauty of a place is not tainted by human interference and remains one that visitors can enjoy in all its glory. In my opinion, these people are the unsung heroes of the National Trust, who blend into their surroundings so well that they often go unnoticed by those who visit. This book is particularly indebted to the wardens Jon Brookes at West Penwith, Alastair Cameron at the Lizard and Geoff Hann at Studland.

Thanks are also due to Jacky Ferneyhough, Hugo Blomfield, Jo Burgon, John Harvey, Janet Lister and Hilary Moorcroft, who all played their part in creating this beautiful book.

Richard Offen
Neptune Coastline Campaign Manager
January, 2003

History

The National Trust owns coastal properties throughout England, Wales and Northern Ireland, and thus a wide geological range. The land beneath us, of course, affects the landscape, provides natural history habitats and the resources for mining and quarrying.

Nowhere is the geology more dramatic than on the Giant's Causeway on Northern Ireland's Antrim coast. The extraordinary basalt columns sparked off a debate that raged politely throughout the eighteenth century, mostly amongst clergymen who seem to have enjoyed a virtual monopoly of the study of geology. Engravings of the stone encouraged visitors, including Dr Johnson, who famously declared that the Causeway was worth seeing, but not worth *going* to see.

Man's impact on the coast can be traced through the centuries, from ancient field systems and burial mounds to lighthouses and military remains. The political survival, and ultimately the wealth enjoyed by Britain's islands, depended on being able to defend the coasts against foreign incursions, first from the Scandinavians, later the Spanish, Dutch and French – and, at times, the Scots. Dunstanburgh Castle in Northumbria (opposite), for instance, was strengthened by John of Gaunt in the late fourteenth century as a barrier against the Scots, though soon afterwards it was a key fortress in the English Wars of the Roses.

Corfe Castle in Dorset represents a site of great strategic importance, with a long and violent history. The present castle was built by William the Conqueror and strengthened by King John in 1204 after he had lost Normandy to his French cousin. Bad King John imprisoned his niece in fine new quarters while starving her knights to death in a dungeon. The castle's end came in the seventeenth century, during the Civil War, when the brave chatelaine, Mary Bankes, was forced to surrender through treachery.

Orford Ness in Suffolk is a reminder of a much more recent past. The flat terrain and isolated situation proved ideal for military purposes, so from the First World War through to the end of the Cold War, trials for radar, bombs and ultimately nuclear warhead detonators were carried out here. In 1993 the National Trust was able to buy a five-mile stretch of the shingle spit, and return it to an area of wilderness, although the structures of war will remain as a disturbing backdrop to the landscape.

previous page: One of the beaches at Upper Solva in Dyfed. In pre-Cambrian times, over 570 million years ago, the volcanic landscape was flooded by the sea, leaving sediments that are full of fossils, including the giant trilobites that are a feature of the Solva area.

opposite: looking south from Kynance Cove on the Lizard Peninsula, in south Cornwall.

above right: Bosigran in West Penwith on Cornwall's north coast. Four hundred million years ago, Cornwall's rocks were being laid down in a shallow ocean. Massive earth movements crumpled these mudstones, sandstones and lavas, raising them up into mountains. From a huge depth, granite was forced upwards by intense heat and pressure, turning some of the sediments into slate. At the same time, liquids and gases containing metals were injected along fractures, and solidified in the cooler conditions. Erosion over the millennia reduced the mountains to the undulating landscape shown here, and revealed the mineral veins that have provided Cornwall's industry.

below left & right: Further north up the Cornish coast, at Sandy Mouth near Bude, the geology is much softer. Beneath the shallow cap of soil, clay and broken stones are the massive rocks of the 'Bude Formation', created about 300 million years ago when the area lay beneath the sea. Layers of fine sand and silt dropped to the ocean floor, gradually compacting to become sandstones and shales. A million years later, molten magma was forced up from the earth's core through the sedimentary rocks, to form the granite hills of Bodmin Moor and Dartmoor. Some of the molten rock spread in a gigantic molten sheet, distorting the local rocks into twisted formations, as can be seen here at Sandy Mouth.

opposite, left: The beach at Horden on the Durham coast. This landscape is created by the magnesian limestone laid down 240 million years ago, during the Permian period. It is formed from the remains of skeletons and shells of creatures that built reefs or settled on the bed of a tropical sea. Magnesian limestone rarely appears close to the surface in Britain, and it is even rarer for such outcrops to exist near the sea.

Earlier in geological history the area was covered in forest and swamps. The subsequent burial of the forests led to the extensive coal deposits that now lie beneath the limestone plateau. Because the coal layers under the sea were comparatively easy to exploit, the coastal area between the rivers Wear and Tees has been an industrial site for centuries.

Sandstone boulders on the beach at East Ebb, part of the Golden Cap Estate in Dorset (above). This eight-mile stretch of coast is made up of blue lias clays capped with green sandstone (opposite, right), which becomes a golden colour in sunshine. The area is so important geologically that in 2002 the Dorset coast became a World Heritage Site.

opposite: Seacombe Cliffs on the Isle of Purbeck in Dorset. Among the rocks of the Purbeck coastal area are those of crystalline limestone that can be polished to look like marble. Purbeck 'marble' comes from two seams of hard limestone, one grey-green, the other red, and has been quarried on the coast between Seacombe and St Aldhem's Head since Roman times (see pp.46–7).

right: Further east on the Dorset coast are the chalk cliffs and pinnacles of Harry Rocks and Ballard Point. The seam runs from the south coast of Dorset and continues through to the Isle of Wight, ending with the Needles. It was formed in the Cretaceous period, between 144 and 65 million years ago. The coast at Harry Rocks has suffered from the work of marine organisms and some grinding away of the chalk by sand and pebbles. Old Harry, probably named after the Devil, sadly lost his wife in 1896 when she was destroyed by the sea.

opposite and right: Robin Hood's Bay in North Yorkshire, showing the cliffs of Oolitic limestone, dating from the Jurassic period, 200 million years ago. Oolite is made up of spherical particles of calcite, producing a dry terrain with streams vanishing from the surface into caverns. These proved very useful in the eighteenth and nineteenth centuries, when smuggling flourished here. In the fishing village of Robin Hood's Bay, smuggled goods could pass up through the caverns into the cellars of the houses: it is said that a bale of cotton could go from the bottom to the top of the village without seeing daylight.

opposite and right: Whitepark Bay
in County Antrim. The chalk cliffs that
sweep around the golden sand mark a
distinct change from the tilted basalt
stacks of Carrick-a-Rede at the eastern
end of the bay, and the cliffs of the
Causeway coast (pp.28–9) to the west.
The variety of plants and habitats
reflect the underlying rocks: the sand
dunes provide refuge for plants such as
sea sandwort, agrimony and spurges;
the chalk grassland maintains a wide
range of wild flowers and grasses; and
the shaded slopes below the cliff favour
a variety of woodland plants, such as
wood anemone and primrose.

The chalk cliffs of Kent represent one of the symbolic landscapes of Britain. Here the North Downs run into the English Channel, and the cliffs are formed from the fossil remains of myriads of microscopic sea creatures that settled at the bottom of the ocean over 100 million years ago. This is the nearest point to mainland Europe, and sharp-eyed Romans, looking out from the shores of Gaul, noted the brilliant white of the cliffs in sunshine and called the mysterious island Albion from *alba*, the Latin for white. Silica in the chalk forms as bands of flint, and has been used as a building material over the centuries in this unwooded area: for instance, for the castles at Dover and Pevensey, and for local parish churches.

The photograph opposite shows Langdon Cliffs, a haven of peace and natural beauty after the clamour of the docks at Dover. Further west, it is the turn of the South Downs to run into the sea, producing the spectacular sweep of the Seven Sisters in East Sussex (above), seen here in winter.

The Giant's Causeway, one of the most spectacular features of the Antrim coast. It was formed 60 million years ago when volcanic activity caused the earlier chalk landscape to be covered by layers of lava. As the top layer lost its heat, regular cracks were created to produce polygonal columns that now look strange, even man-made. In all, there are 40,000 of these columns on the Irish coast, with a similar formation on the Scottish island of Staffa.

The picture opposite shows part of the Causeway looking east; in the picture on the right, the photographer's daughter provides a scale for the columns of the feature known as the Organ.

The Giant's Causeway was unknown to the rest of the world until 1694, when Dr Samuel Foley, Bishop of Down and Connor, wrote a paper for the Royal Society that included a drawing of the stones. This instigated a scientific debate with the protagonists dividing themselves into Neptunists and Vulcanists. Neptunists believed that the phenomenon of the Causeway was the result of particles in the seawater settling on the seabed and becoming first mud and then columns. The Vulcanists plumped for a volcanic origin, and they were eventually proved right.

opposite, above: Coastal retreat and strong tides at Formby on Merseyside often uncover ancient prints – semi-fossilised hoofprints of auroch, red deer and roe deer which grazed the salt-marshes in Neolithic times, and human footprints. But these huge prints, here being inspected by National Trust volunteer Gordon Roberts and his dog Kim, are very ancient indeed – dinosaur footprints.

opposite, below: Rhossili Down on the eastern tip of the Gower Peninsula in Wales is the site of a variety of prehistoric remains, including cairns, stone circles, early field enclosures and, as here, Neolithic burial chambers.

above left: West Penwith, a rectangle of land that starts at St Ives and stretches along the north coast of Cornwall down to Cape Cornwall and Lands End, was described by the artist Barbara Hepworth as a pagan landscape and it gave form to many of her sculptures. Farms are dotted across rocky headlands, their pattern of stone walls and little fields surviving from the Iron Age.

above: The early settlers on the Gower Peninsula named the Worms Head from its resemblance to a dragon – 'wurm' is the Old English for dragon or serpent. The lumpy limestone promontory rears forward like the head of a dragon, drawing its sinuous coils behind it.

left: The Vile on Rhossili Down, showing the ancient strip farming system. 'Vile' is Old English for field, and this is the best preserved medieval field system in Britain, with the farmers still growing their crops in narrow strips known as landshares.

opposite, above: One of the burial mounds at Sutton Hoo in Suffolk. During an archaeological dig here just before the outbreak of the Second World War, this mound yielded up a magnificent ship burial, probably that of Raedwald, King of the East Angles, who died c. AD625.

opposite, below left: Braich-y-Pwll in Gwynedd, showing the ancient field systems divided up by stone walls called *claddu*. In the distance can be seen Bardsey Island, or Ynys Enlli, the Island of Twenty Thousand Saints. One of the first monastic settlements in Britain, it was founded by St Cadfan in AD430, and in the Middle Ages became a major pilgrimage centre. Those who made the pilgrimage could claim the equivalent of reaching Rome.

opposite, below right: A granite stack on Lundy, an island set in the Bristol Channel. It has been home to settlers since the Stone Age, and provided a haven for the Vikings and more recent vistors. Lundy is an archaeological paradise, while the seas around it comprise England's only statutory marine nature reserve.

The Cornish coast abounds with legends about King Arthur and Camelot. Loe Pool (above), a lagoon in Mount's Bay, has been identified as the magical lake into which Sir Bedivere threw Excalibur. Barras Nose (right) is a rocky headland on the north coast, overlooked by Tintagel Castle. Interest in all matters Arthurian became intense in the nineteenth century, and the threat of King Arthur's Castle being built on the headland prompted local people to raise a subscription of £500 to present Barras Nose to the infant National Trust in 1897.

opposite: St Michael's Mount is a rocky island in Mount's Bay, off the south coast of Cornwall, which can only be reached on foot at low tide. It became a pilgrimage centre in the fifth century, when St Michael appeared to a local fisherman: the shrine was enhanced by the arrival of the jawbone of St Appolonia, which was believed to cure toothache. In 1070, Robert, Count of Mortain, gave the island to the Benedictines, and it became a daughter house of Mont St Michel, 150 miles across the Channel. At the dissolution of the monasteries, the Mount became first a fortress and then the home of the St Aubyn family after the English Civil War.

right and next page: The ruins of Corfe Castle are set dramatically on a steep hill, with the village clinging around their base. It is a site of great strategic importance, as the castle stands on a mound that forms part of the main chalk ridge running east to west across the Isle of Purbeck, on the south Dorset coast. Two rivers cut through the ridge, creating the mound, and the name Corfe is derived from the Old English for a gap or cutting. Here William the Conqueror built a castle that survived intact until it fell to parliamentary forces during the English Civil War. The castle was then slighted to prevent it being used in war again, and now stands as a picturesque ruin.

opposite, above left & right: Lindisfarne Castle on Holy Island off the Northumbrian coast was built in the 1540s as part of England's defence against the Scots, but its military use was short-lived. The decaying fort was discovered by Edward Hudson, the founder of *Country Life*, who commissioned the architect Edwin Lutyens to turn it into a summer retreat (p.95).

opposite, below right: In July 1588, as the Spanish Armada sailed into the English Channel and threatened invasion, a string of beacons was created across the country as an early warning system. In the event, the Spanish fleet was defeated at Gravelines on 8 August and forced to flee. To celebrate the four hundredth anniversary, beacons were lit throughout England in August 1988. This photograph shows the lighting of the beacon on the Golden Cap Estate in Dorset.

above: Another century, and another threat of invasion, this time from the French. Lord Palmerston's aggressive foreign policy brought about the prospect of war in 1858. The Needles Old Battery was built on the south-west tip of the Isle of Wight to guard the approach to the Solent and the major naval base at Portsmouth.

right: Wreckage on the shore of Barafundle Bay in Dyfed, with Stackpole Head in the distance.

Stretching ten miles south of Aldeburgh in Suffolk is the narrow shingle spit of Orford Ness. It runs parallel with the mainland, separated from it by the River Ore, which it forces ever further south. For centuries, Orford provided vital shelter from the winter storms that swept in from the North Sea, but as tidal changes caused the river to silt up and the spit to form, so the harbour lost its importance as one of the great ports of the east coast (top right). Instead, a lighthouse was erected on the Ness itself in the sixteenth century. This was replaced in 1792 by the present lighthouse, Upper Light, which can be seen looking west across Stoney Ditch (opposite).

In the twentieth century, the Ness took on quite a different life. The flat terrain and isolated situation proved ideal for military purposes; in the 1930s, trials for radar were conducted here and in the Second World War Barnes Wallis experimented with new types of bomb (previous page). With the Cold War, aerials were established on the Cobra Mist site, providing a sophisticated defence system for gathering information. Pagodas for testing nuclear warhead detonators gave Orford Ness a strangely exotic skyline (right).

opposite: Blakeney Point on the north Norfolk coast. The loneliness and mystery of the sea creeks and mud-flats fascinated the writer Jack Higgins and inspired his famous novel, *The Eagle Has Landed*, about a German plan to assassinate Winston Churchill while he was staying in Norfolk in the autumn of 1943.

above: West Wheal Owles and Wheal Edward engine houses on the headland of Kenidjack, Cape Cornwall. The remains of tin-mining dominate this landscape, and the great boom time in this part of the world was the middle of the nineteenth century. Reminders of the harshness of the miners' lives are constant. Many had to walk several miles to get to the pits, climb down the shafts by ladder, sometimes to below the level of the sea, then walk a couple of miles to the face.

right: A tin-mine engine house at Carn Galver in the Porthmeor Valley on West Penwith. A revolution took place in the industry when Richard Trevithick invented a steam engine that could pump out water, making it possible to have much deeper mine shafts.

Acton (above) and Norman's (below) quarries on the Isle of Purbeck, Dorset. Purbeck marble has been quarried here since Roman times, but became internationally famous in the Middle Ages when the Crusaders returned from the Holy Land with a taste for marble. The first use of Purbeck marble in London was for the building of the Temple Church, *c.* 1160. The hundreds of fossils in the limestone give the stone a flecked appearance that makes it a particularly attractive stone for pillars, and soon other churches followed the Temple's lead: the cathedrals of Canterbury, Winchester and Salisbury, for example. But it was for tomb effigies that the marble was particularly favoured. King John, who was fond of the Isle of Purbeck as his hunting forest, had his effigy made in the stone for his tomb in Worcester Cathedral.

above: The Peak Alum Works at Ravenscar at the south end of Robin Hood's Bay in North Yorkshire. The first reference to extractions of alum date from the seventeenth century, making it the first chemical industry in England. The rock was roasted slowly over a brushwood fire, and the brick-red residue was then washed with water, and with stale urine. In the words of the London merchant, Daniel Colwell, who visited Ravenscar in 1670, 'the best urine comes from poor labouring people who drink little strong drink'. The alum was then used as a mordant in the dyeing industry.

The village of Porthdinllaen on the Llŷn Peninsula. As the only truly sheltered harbour on Llŷn's north coast, it was a busy little port – records indicate that in 1861 around eight hundred vessels entered here. Its days as a commercial fishing port are over, but it has retained its charm. Things might have been very different if it had secured the packet steamer trade to Ireland. Porthdinllaen, whose geology gave it the perfect deep-sea harbour for the trade, was in competition with Holyhead, but lost by one vote in Parliament. It is still asserted by some that Holyhead swapped the geological specimens thus clinching the decision.

opposite: South Foreland Lighthouse on the
White Cliffs of Dover in Kent. It was built in
1843 to help sailors navigate the treacher-
ous Goodwin Sands. Originally lit by oil,
it later became the first electrically powered
lighthouse in the British Isles. Once out
of sight of land, however, ships were still
entirely isolated until Marconi, using radio
transmission, carried out the first ship-
to-shore demonstration from South Foreland
to the East Goodwin lightship, a distance
of twelve miles, in December 1898.

above: The wreck of the *Preussan*, a sailing
ship that ran aground in 1910 below
Langdon Cliffs.

right: Souter Lighthouse, Tyne and Wear.
Built in 1870, it was the first lighthouse to
be powered by generated electric current,
with its own steam engine and generating
plant. It was also the first to be fitted with
prismatic light as an aid to navigation. Ships
entering the River Wear would be warned
by a red light that they were steering
towards the rocks, while the white light
acted as reassurance that they were on
the correct course.

Haven

As a bird would see it, flying in on a northerly wind from the Arctic, the British coastline offers a host of enticing opportunities. From spectacular rocky headlands to sandy bays and muddy salt-marshes, the diverse coastal landscapes that have resulted from Britain's complex geological evolution provide suitable habitats for a vast range of wildlife. Nor are these habitats static; they are constantly changing and evolving. Although occasionally dramatic, the natural processes of coastal development and change are generally slow, and resident wildlife is usually able to adjust and react accordingly. Other changes, mainly those prompted by the activities of man, can be less subtle, however, and can have an immediate and lasting impact on wildlife habitats. The discovery of the seaside by the Victorians, for example, spawned a long period of development along our coasts that resulted in the loss of many wonderful natural stretches of coastal landscape of great value to wildlife. Now, however, the tide has turned – quite literally – and although certain pressures continue, most coastal sites of wildlife interest are protected, many of them by the National Trust.

In a quite obvious sense the coast is frontier land, the boundary between land and sea. As such it represents a unique crossroads, at which species that are more usually tied to one or other environment may converge. Many different routes meet at this crossroads. For migrating birds the coastline serves as a navigational aid, its habitats as vital pit-stops on the long route to and from more distant parts. For other, more sedentary species, their often very particular needs may be met only in coastal habitats, and in surprisingly specific niches that we may as yet imperfectly understand. Other species will take advantage of the coast only at certain seasons or in particular conditions, such as the kittiwake (opposite), which comes to coastal cliffs only to breed. Whatever their requirements, the many thousands of species of plant, invertebrate, bird and mammal find a vast reserve in our coastline.

The diversity offered by Britain's coasts and seas supports much varied wildlife, from tiny invertebrates to the second biggest cetacean in the world, the fin whale. The minke whale (opposite, top left), regularly recorded off western coasts in summer, is best looked for from headlands and offshore islands. Perhaps easier to see are Britain's populations of dolphins and seals. Several schools of bottle-nosed dolphin and common dolphin (opposite, top right) are resident in British waters, with Cardigan Bay and the Pembrokeshire coast in summer offering an excellent chance of seeing them. The Cornish coast is a great place to look for basking sharks (opposite, centre right), while internationally significant numbers of two species of seal, the common (opposite, below right) and the grey (opposite, centre left) occur on and around Blakeney Point in Norfolk (opposite, below left), where several hundred can sometimes be seen hauled out on the beaches.

Sea mammals may be dramatic, but they are only one part of an enormous ecological jigsaw. Much of the natural history interest around our coasts centres on small marine creatures, such as acorn barnacles (above), limpets (right, centre) and mussels (far right). Beachcombing can yield a wealth of riches: a collection of objects as diverse as a mermaid's purse (top centre), empty razor shell (top right) and washed-up jellyfish (right).

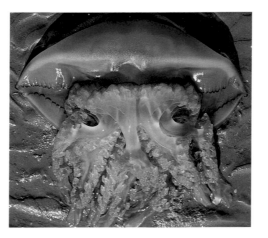

Much beloved of children and devotees of rock-pool exploration, crabs are enduringly fascinating. Seventy or so species are found in Britain, living in a range of coastal habitats from muddy estuaries through sandy beaches to the dark ocean floor. Among the most distinctive species is the edible crab (opposite), best identified by its black-tipped claws and still much prized as a commercial commodity. Crabs have earned a reputation, at least partly true, of being the rubbish collectors of sea and shore. They are certainly scavengers, and are constantly on patrol in search of scraps of food, ranging from dead fish to plant matter.

right: The dramatic seaweed beds of Strangford Lough in Northern Ireland, an outstanding place for wildlife. Much of this interest stems from the 80,000 million gallons of seawater that pour into the lough with each tide, sweeping in untold numbers of invertebrates and thereby replenishing the food supply for the huge flocks of wildfowl, gulls and wading birds that gather here. Impressive numbers of oystercatcher, curlew, redshank, wigeon and teal over-winter at Strangford, along with two-thirds of the world's population of pale-bellied brent geese. It is also one of the best sites in Northern Ireland for spotting otters.

Coastal factors such as salt spray and seemingly incessant onshore winds can have a defining effect on maritime vegetation. Clifftop heaths such as on Holdstone Down, Exmoor (opposite), are composed almost exclusively of so-called dwarf vegetation, mainly heather and gorse, trimmed and sculpted by the elements. Shrubs and trees cannot grow in such an exposed spot, and so wildlife must make do with the limited shelter offered by the clipped stands of heather. The maritime habitats of the Lizard in Cornwall are one of Britain's foremost botanical locations, with many nationally rare species recorded there. Equally, the windswept Atlantic valleys of Cornwall and Devon were among the last British haunts of the large blue butterfly, extinct since 1979 but now successfully reintroduced onto National Trust land.

Protecting her nest from the elements is a major consideration for this female eider duck (right). Effective camouflage will help her escape the attentions of passing gulls and birds of prey, and she will have lined her nest with down plucked from her own breast. When leaving the nest to feed she will pull this down over the eggs and chicks to prevent them from chilling in the wind and to help hide them from predators.

Warm, south-facing ledges and slopes are likely places to seek out reptiles, such as the adder (opposite). With the backdrop of an azure sea, and dramatic red valerian either side of the basking snake, this image seems more akin to a scene in the Mediterranean than to one in Devon, where this photograph was taken. Our climate is not ideal for these sun-loving creatures, but mild, sheltered sites on the coast are suitable for adders and common lizards, whilst natterjack toads can be seen in pools among the coastal sand dunes of the National Trust's reserve at Formby, near Liverpool.

One of the most colourful displays of coastal flora is provided by thrift or sea pink (right). Thrift is a real survivor, growing as readily on cushions of grassy turf as in crevices between rocks, and is widely distributed around British coasts in a range of habitats. The colour of the flower is as variable as its flowering season is long – from as early as March (in sheltered parts of Cornwall) through to early September – and ranges from deep pink to almost white.

Coastal flora and fauna exhibit a rich kaleido-scope of colours and textures. In autumn the bar-tailed godwit (opposite) loses its rich cinna-mon-coloured breeding plumage in favour of a much more subtle but equally attractive range of beige and buff tints, with almost every feather delicately outlined. Many thousands of these birds descend on Britain in winter, having nested on the tundra of the high Arctic. They mix readily with other waders, forming huge flocks in locations like the Wash and the Thames estuary.

Some of the most interesting tones and textures are only revealed temporarily, as with kelp, here exposed at low tide (above, left). Attached to the rocks by root-like branches that extend from the base of its stalk, kelp is widely distributed around rocky coasts and its extensive fan-shaped fronds can form dense mats of floating vegetation. The rich green colour and shiny texture are soon lost on the detached fragments that end up deposited on beaches after storms. Sea campion (above), however, is always on display, bobbing in the wind and often growing in association with thrift on exposed clifftops and slopes.

Winter in Britain may be harsh at times, but it is infinitely preferable to conditions further north. To escape the ice and snow of Scandinavia and Arctic Russia, many thousands of redshanks head south in autumn, crowding our estuaries and coastal marshes until it is time to fly north again in early spring. A nervous and noisy bird, it is almost always the first species to start calling at the approach of danger, and so acts as a useful sentinel for large, mixed flocks of waders when there are predators like peregrine falcon in the vicinity. Redshanks also breed in Britain, although in much reduced numbers, due to drainage and disturbance. Where our native birds spend the winter is not entirely clear, although there is evidence that some may move south to France and Iberia.

Life on the cliffs is not easy, yet many species make a virtue of necessity. Kittiwakes (opposite) set up home in the most death-defying locations, their compact nest of seaweed scraps perched precariously on the very brink of a ledge. This seeming reluctance to get to real grips with *terra firma* is not entirely surprising, as kittiwakes spend most of the year far out at sea, only returning to land for a few weeks in spring and summer in

order to breed. This they do in large colonies, notable for the incessant and deafening cries of 'kitt-ee-wayke', the call from which the bird – a type of gull – gets its name.

above: Sheltered rock crevices are excellent places to seek out plants like the English stonecrop. With little available fresh water, and a high salt factor in the soil and air, only

certain plants can survive in such locations. The stonecrop's fleshy leaves help to conserve moisture, shallow roots make the most of what little soil or sand is present, and the plants' generally prostrate habit ensures they make the most of the shelter (and warmth, when the sun is shining) that the rocks provide.

Among the most dramatic spectacles of our coasts are the enormous flocks of wading birds that gather here in winter. These number many thousands of birds, in flocks of up to 50,000 individuals of twenty or so different species. The knot, often seen packed tightly in vast numbers on mudflats or in flight, is an awesome sight, with the birds changing direction simultaneously in a split second, flashing their silver under parts as they turn. In summer, however, the knot sheds its grey winter colours and takes on a rufous hue; the photograph opposite was taken in early spring, when some of the knot were already assuming their breeding plumage prior to their return migration northwards. Also on view are a few dunlin, a smaller wader that shares the knot's nesting grounds beyond the Arctic Circle.

right: A black-tailed godwit, one of Britain's scarcer waders, in summer plumage. Slightly larger and rather more elegant than its bar-tailed relative (see p.64), this species does not occur here in such large numbers, although it is a regular winter visitor to estuaries such as the Dee on the Welsh/English border and the Exe in Devon.

opposite: The coastline of Wales is among the most dramatic of anywhere in the British Isles, with a huge range of habitats amid breathtaking scenery. The island of Grassholm supports a range of nesting seabirds, including one of the largest colonies of gannet in the northern hemisphere. This was not always so. Indeed, in the mid-nineteenth century there were very few pairs of gannet present on the island, but a few decades later numbers had increased enough to prompt the fisher-men of Milford Haven to call for the birds' destruction, on the grounds of the threat they posed to local fish stocks. This move was thankfully resisted, and the gannet colony now numbers 32,000 pairs. In late summer, with the young of the year present, there may be as many as 100,000 gannets on the island.

right: The rocky nature of the National Trust's Stackpole Estate makes it ideal for the more retiring wildlife species, including seals, which take advantage of the caves in which to have their pups. Crevice-nesting birds such as the chough (see p.79) and storm petrel will also choose such inaccessible locations as breeding sites.

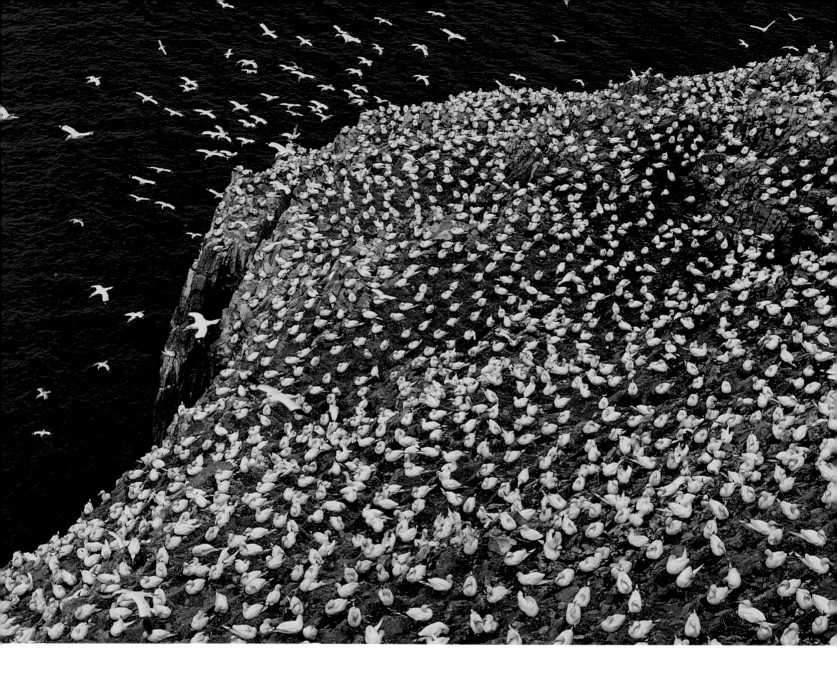

Gannets en masse at Bass Rock, at the mouth of the Firth of Forth (opposite). This huge gannetry is one of the most famous in Britain, and from a distance in summer looks as though it is capped with snow, so densely covered is it by nesting birds. However, closer examination reveals that each sitting bird is at a critical distance – the range of a stretch and stab of the beak – from its neighbour. Human visitors need to be mindful of the gannet's powerful bill, but a greater trial is coping with the overwhelming stench created by the birds' droppings.

right: Limpets and a fossilised ammonite on rocks at Ravenscar in North Yorkshire. The coast is a great place to go fossil-hunting, and careful examination of rock surfaces will reveal all sorts of interesting evidence of ancient animal life. The beach below the Undercliff at Lyme Regis in Dorset is one of the most celebrated fossil and dinosaur sites of all, thanks to the endeavours of nineteenth-century palaeontologists such as Mary and Joseph Anning.

Like some sort of seabird Manhattan, rock skyscrapers populated with guillemots, kittiwakes and shags rise up from the waters off the Northumberland coast. The Farne Islands are home to some of Britain's foremost seabird colonies, and famed worldwide for the relatively confiding nature of the birds that live there. Public access is strictly controlled to ensure that this very special quality is not lost, giving visitors views they would normally only get through a telescope. The numbers of birds breeding on the Farnes are awesome: more than twenty different species nest here, including 34,000 pairs of puffin, 22,000 pairs of guillemot, 6,000 pairs of kittiwake and several hundred pairs of tern (of four species). The islands' location also makes them a convenient landfall for a wide range of migratory birds, including rarities blown over from Scandinavia in autumn.

Also present on the Farnes is the eider duck (see p.61). The much-revered monk St Cuthbert, who died here in AD687, was an avid protector of the eiders and set out clear rules and regulations concerning their preservation. The birds subsequently became known as St Cuthbert's ducks, and continue to breed on the islands today.

Most species of seabird nest colonially and at high densities, with every available ledge seemingly occupied (opposite). In such crowded situations, it is sometimes difficult to consider individual species more closely. The razorbill (above), is closely related to the guillemot and looks similar, but it has jet black rather than dark brown upper parts and a much more extravagant beak.

One of the rarest coastal birds in Britain is the chough (above right). Closely associated with the heraldry and folklore of Cornwall, the species has only recently returned to breed in the county after an absence of half a century. The British population of cormorant (right), meanwhile, continues to strengthen, although there are still relatively few nesting colonies, almost all of which are coastal.

The iconic status of the puffin is surely due in no small part to its faintly comical appearance and stature. Like portly waiters, puffins stand around near their nesting burrows, shuffling about and uttering their strange, faintly ridiculous, chuckling calls. Flying looks an effort for them, their fat bodies propelled by furiously flapping wings. Underwater, however, they are superbly efficient hunting machines, zipping along at speeds approaching fifty miles per hour, and very adept at chasing and catching the small fish on which they feed. The colourful bill, which has doubtless helped earn the puffin its other name of sea parrot, is a spring and summer event only, used for display and in courtship. In winter the bright colours subside, although the triangular shape remains distinctive.

Puffins like to nest in old rabbit burrows and, where there is ample habitat and plentiful food, can form extensive colonies. Overall, however, their numbers are currently showing signs of decline, especially in the south. For example, they were traditionally associated with Lundy, in the Bristol Channel, and appeared famously on the island's stamps. Sadly, however, there are no more than a handful of pairs remaining on Lundy today.

[81]

Britain's coast supports vast populations of gulls, including two species of 'black-backs', the greater and the lesser (opposite, above). Identification is essentially down to size – the greater is bigger – and leg colour: the greater's are pink, the lesser's yellow. Great opportunists, they will also feast on amphibians such as the rare natterjack toad (opposite, below), the conservation of which is a high priority nationally.

With such varied wildlife living along our coasts, survey work (above) is essential to see how different species are faring and what action might be required to assist those in decline. Surveying wildlife is not always easy. Birds, clearly, are highly mobile and some species are not wholly dependent on the coast. The grey heron (left) will move regularly between a whole range of habitats, both inland and coastal.

[83]

Coastal flora must withstand testing conditions. Securing a sheltered site is often not an option, so some species, such as the sea pea (opposite) have evolved to thrive right out in the open, in this case on the shingle of Orford Ness in Suffolk. However, such brazen habits can expose the plants to other risks. Among these is the fate often suffered by the sea holly (above), too frequently taken for use in floral decorations, or dug up for transplanting to a garden. Such activities have caused its virtual disappearance in some locations. Sea kale (above right) was traditionally gathered for different reasons: it was good to eat. The young shoots were highly prized, and cut and sent to market by the cartload. No such fate awaited the yellow-horned poppy (right), however. All parts of the plant are toxic, which perhaps helps explain its continued presence along many of our coasts.

Many coastal gardens in Devon and Cornwall provide a haven for exotic and tender plants that would not survive or prosper elsewhere in Britain. Glendurgan (previous page), on the Helford River, is a 'classic' Cornish garden, with a steep wooded valley running down to the shore, allowing frost to 'drain' away to the sea. The main problem here would be gales, so Alfred Fox, creator of the garden in the 1820s, erected shelterbelts of deciduous trees and conifers. This enables rhododendrons and azaleas to flourish in the early spring.

Overbecks lies on the Devon Riviera, with appropriately sub-tropical conditions. Otto Overbecks, writing of his garden in 1933, exclaimed: 'It is so warm and beautiful here. I grow Bananas, Oranges and Pomegranates in the open garden, and have 3,000 palm trees, planted out in my woods and garden.' The view towards Salcombe and the sea (left) shows some of the exotic summer plants. The parterre (above) is planted up with orange trees.

previous page: Trelissick lies on the south Cornish coast, on the banks of the River Fal. Channels Creek can be glimpsed through the bare trees of the woodland garden in early spring.

right: The stream garden at Coleton Fishacre on the south Devon coast. This provides a comfortable home for moisture-loving and marginal plants including hostas, candelabra primulas, bluebells and irises. Exbury hybrid azaleas give fragrance in early May.

opposite, above & below: Trengwainton, near Penzance in the far south-western corner of Cornwall. The creator of the gardens, Sir Rose Price, derived his wealth from his family's Jamaican sugar plantations, and the results are equally exotic, with phormiums, bamboos and grasses, and camellias providing colour in January.

opposite: Detail of the 'candle' of the tall *Echium Pininana*, a native of Madeira, in the garden at Coleton Fishacre.

It is very rare to find a great country house on the coast. Castles there are a-plenty, but they were built for defence. Our ancestors did not regard the coast as the ideal place to set their estates. Indeed, when Abbot Upcher suggested to the landscape architect Humphry Repton that his new house at Sheringham Park should have views of the sea, Repton dissuaded him, pointing out that a sea view might be pleasant in the Bay of Naples, but not in the harsh climate of the north Norfolk coast: 'In considering Sheringham as a permanent residence, and not as a mere summer villa, we must recollect how it may appear in winter.'

Edwin Lutyens may well have felt the same when he was asked by Edward Hudson to transform the ruined Tudor fort of Lindisfarne Castle off the Northumberland coast into a home. He succeeded magnificently, as can be seen in this photograph of the Ship Room (left). Nevertheless, Lindisfarne was intended as a summer retreat; only the indomitable housekeeper stayed here in the winter months.

opposite: The Stackpole estate lies on the south Welsh coast in Dyfed. For three centuries it was owned by the Scottish earls of Cawdor, who built a classical mansion and land-scaped the estate by planting woodlands and damming valleys to make freshwater lakes. The engraving above shows the rear façade of the largely redesigned Victorian house, with the lake and the Eight-Arch Bridge. In 1963 the house was demolished, leaving only the service quarters; when the National Trust acquired Stackpole fourteen years later, these buildings were converted to provide a residential base camp for school parties that come each year to enjoy various sports and study nature conservation (see pp.116–17).

Frederick Augustus Hervey, Bishop of Derry and later 4th Earl of Bristol, chose to build his mansion, Downhill, on a bleak headland on the Ulster coast. Hervey, known to posterity as the Bishop Earl, was a wildly unconventional character, whose way of dispensing livings to his curates was to organise running races along the sands. He began to build Downhill in about 1775, with the help of the Irish architect, Michael Shanahan.

The house is now a bleak ruin in the middle of a landscape park that the Earl Bishop had created out of moorland. But the glory of Downhill is the charming Mussenden Temple, perched on the very edge of the cliffs. Hervey had a passion for rotundas, and designed his English house, Ickworth in Suffolk, as a central rotunda with flanking wings. The Mussenden Temple is supported by Corinthian columns, with an

urn crowning the top. It was intended as a commemoration of another of his passions, his cousin Frideswide Mussenden, twenty years old, married, very pretty and virtuous. Sadly it was also to be her memorial, as she died suddenly in 1785.

Work and Play

The idea of the coast as a place of leisure and fun is a comparatively recent one. For our ancestors, it was a place of work, of pitting man against nature, and of extracting a living out of often meagre resources.

The early inhabitants of West Penwith on the northern coast of Cornwall, for instance, combined three industries to sustain themselves: farming, fishing and mining. From the late eighteenth century until the early 1900s, the main fishing catch was pilchards. Huers, stationed on the headlands, would alert the community when vast shoals of the fish, flashing silver in the water, suddenly appeared. The tin-miners came up from their shafts, and the farmers downed their tools to rush to their seine boats.

The departure of the pilchard shoals was as dramatic as their arrivals – the industry died as a result of over-fishing. This is a continuing story, with the fishing industry in decline all around Britain's coasts – the fishermen shown in the following photographs face an uncertain future.

Instead of a place of work, the coast has become a huge adventure playground. The first, tentative steps towards this began in the mid-seventeenth century when a doctor in Scarborough in Yorkshire declared that drinking seawater could cure illnesses such as scurvy, jaundice and leprosy. The drinking palled but bathing took off, and seaside resorts developed, encouraged by the patronage of George III at Weymouth in Dorset, and of the Prince Regent in Brighton, Sussex. Steam trains and the establishment of bank holidays made seaside trips possible for the less well-off, although it is sobering to realise that the Holidays with Pay Act was only passed in 1938. The seaside holiday of fond childhood memories had arrived.

Now many fly abroad in search of sunshine, and there has been a dramatic downturn in the numbers opting for the British coast as their main holiday. Instead, beaches and beautiful coastland provide leisure activities for short breaks – walking, canoeing, hang-gliding, or simply mucking about with bucket and spade.

previous page: A fisherman loading his boat up ready to go fishing for lobster and crab off Cape Cornwall. The state of cove fishing, using hand lines and pots, is in dire straits due to EU quota regulations, with Cornish fishermen operating on a small, sustainable scale forced to restrict their catches in line with the limits imposed on the larger vessels leaving the port of Newlyn. There are few young fishermen coming into the industry.

left: Robin Hood's Bay in North Yorkshire has two settlements: the town of Robin Hood's Bay or Bay Town at the northern end, and Ravenscar at the southern. During the nineteenth century, Bay Town was one of the most important fishing ports on the Yorkshire coast: in 1820 there were 130 fishermen working cobles, flat-bottomed, high-bowed boats of Viking ancestry, and five larger ships. Tourism is now the industry of Bay Town, not surprising, given its quaint charm. The National Trust owns the former coastguard station, which has been converted into an education and visitor centre.

Ravenscar is less picturesque; for centuries it has been the site of alum quarries (p.47). In the nineteenth century, however, there was a scheme to turn the headland into another Scarborough. A railway was built, small plots of land allotted and roads and drains laid. But there were few buyers, and the company went bankrupt. Ravenscar is now known as the 'town that never was'.

opposite: The fishing hamlet of Durgan, on the north bank of the Helford River, consists of around twenty cottages, originally occupied by men fishing the pilchards, mackerel, lobster and crab for which the Helford River and Falmouth Bay were renowned. Their catches would be taken into Falmouth market by donkeys, which roamed the fields around Durgan in the summer months, and lived in cellars during the winter.

above: Boscastle on the north Cornish coast is the only safe haven on this stretch of coast. Sailing vessels could not get through the narrow strait without the assistance of 'hobblers', boats with eight oars and men on either shore, using guide ropes to keep the ships in mid-Channel.

above right: Carrying the catch up the steep pathway on Carrick-a-Rede, North Antrim. Carrick-a-Rede is Gaelic for 'Rock on the Road', the road in this case being the one followed by the salmon on their way to spawn in the Antrim rivers. The island is separated from the mainland by a deep chasm, and at the beginning of the fishing season a rope bridge is slung across the chasm.

right: Unloading fish at Mullion Cove, on the west side of the Lizard Peninsula, Cornwall.

A fisherman's life at Cape Cornwall (opposite, top left & right), Penberth Cove, Cornwall (opposite, below left) and Runswick Bay, Yorkshire (opposite, below right). No matter which end of the country, fishermen face similar struggles. At Penberth stocks of crab and lobster are declining, though a scheme to raise young lobsters in Padstow and transport them out to sea provides some prospect of saving the lobster industry. At Runswick Bay the industry is in decline, with the number of boats dropping by a third.

right: Detail of lobster nets at Mullion Cove.

previous page: Cowbar Nab at Staithes in North Yorkshire, the birthplace in 1728 of Captain James Cook, who was apprenticed to a Whitby shipowner before launching himself on his great voyages of exploration.

opposite: The lifeboat station on the Lizard Peninsula in Cornwall. This was built as a result of a local landowner's horror at the appalling wreck of the *Czar* in January 1859, with the loss of 123 lives, including that of the captain, drowned while trying to rescue his wife and five-year-old son, who were trapped in their cabin. Originally the boat-house was at the top of the cove, but the drop was so precipitous that in stormy weather the crew used to crawl down on their hands and knees lest they be flipped over the edge. By the time the station was closed in 1961, the lifeboat had been launched 136 times, and saved 562 lives.

right: A Northumbrian fishing boat moored in harbour. Lindisfarne Castle on Holy Island can be seen in the background. The traditional east-coast fishing for salmon, sea trout, cod, lobster and crab in cobles is very much on the decline. Some boats are licensed by the National Trust to take visitors take visitors out to view seabirds such as puffins and terns, and seals.

opposite: The extraordinary landscape of Strangford Lough in County Down, Northern Ireland. Drumlins, which look like flying saucers, are deposits dumped by the retreating ice sheets at the end of the last Ice Age. These islands, together with the shoreline, provide habitats for a wide range of plant and animal species. Sheep grazing is therefore very important here: as sheep keep the swath low, so small plants are able to flourish.

above: Romney Marsh sheep at Morte Point on the north Devon coast, far from their original home in Kent. This is a good, hardy breed of sheep, known for its excellent meat and wool, the staple in the late Middle Ages that enabled Romney marshes to become an area of considerable prosperity.

opposite: Ponies grazing on the Golden Cap Estate in Dorset. They play a vital part in maintaining a rich grassland community, which is noted for its species of flowers, grasses and butterflies. The ponies eat invasive species such as *bracopodium* that other animals would not appreciate as part of their diet.

above: Cattle at Nanjulian Farm, outside St Just on the West Penwith coast of Cornwall. This farm has recently become organic under National Trust tenancy. Many of the agricultural holdings in Penwith have ceased to be working farms, which can have a detrimental effect on this bleak and rugged landscape, and on its flora and fauna. This is why it is so important that organisations like the Trust encourage the traditions of farming.

Chyngton Farm on the Cuckmere estuary in East Sussex, with
the Seven Sisters providing a dramatic backdrop. The National
Trust leased the farm to a local tenant in 1993, and now new
saltmarshes are being created through managed realignment,
thus ensuring the agricultural legacy of this precious estuary.

The coast as playground. National Trust beaches tend to be in fairly remote places, though there are exceptions. Studland Bay in Poole Harbour in Dorset (opposite, below left) is one. The beach, shown here with windbreaks, attracts over one and a quarter million visitors annually. It is also diminishing in size; erosion is claiming about 1 metre each year.

above: A glider flies over the dramatic chalk cliffs of Seven Sisters, Dorset.

left: Canoeing at Barafundle Bay. Barafundle is part of the Stackpole Estate in Dyfed (pp.94–5). The Activity Centre at Stackpole brings children and young people from inner cities to enjoy the delights of the coast, from rock climbing and abseiling to studying nature conservation.

next page: With the decline of the Northumbrian fishing industry, some of the traditional cobles have been converted into beach huts at Lindisfarne.

Advance and Retreat

Britain's coastline is constantly changing. Smallhythe Place, the home of the great actress Ellen Terry at Tenterden in Kent, is now ten miles from the sea. It is difficult to believe that it started life as the Port House for a thriving shipyard. Dunwich in Suffolk was a major seaport in the Middle Ages. Now, most of its buildings, including several churches, are under the North Sea. Erosion and accretion have always been with us, but now climatic warming is adding the likelihood of storms and erosive swells, resulting in the rise of the sea level.

Legend has it that the Danish king, Canute, tried to hold back the waves. Man has continued along this path by building fortifications and barriers that are usually hugely expensive, and can push the problem on to another part of the coast. This is the lesson learned at West Wittering in Sussex, where protective modifications to shoreline towns have put at risk the future of the sand spit at East Head. On several coastal sites, the National Trust has adopted a policy of managed retreat, an abandonment of a line of defence, allowing a natural water's edge to develop, as at Northey Island in Essex.

Pollution can appear in a whole range of guises, from plastic waste to visible effluent from sewage discharge, posing a serious threat to the maritime fringe. The damage inflicted in 1998 by the oil tanker *Sea Empress* on the Pembrokeshire coast was both devastating and long-lasting. A happier story is provided by the beach at Horden in Durham, polluted over many years by the coal waste dumped from the seams under the sea. The cleansing power of the sea has been extraordinary at this site, and in fifteen years has turned the beach from black to gold.

previous page: The foreshore below Ravenscar, looking out over Robin Hood's Bay, North Yorkshire. Over 70% of the east coast of England, with its comparatively soft rocks, is eroding.

opposite: Beach huts swamped by the sand dunes on the beach at Brancaster in Norfolk. Brancaster and Blakeney Point to the east, with their fluid sand dunes, are undergoing both erosion and accretion as the sand moves from one site to another. The dunes can be stabilised by planting marram grass, but it is important not to spoil natural habitats. At Formby on Merseyside (right), shallow dishes in the sand fill with moisture during winter, and provide warm water breeding sites for the very rare natterjack toad.

next page:
Marram grass at West Wittering, West Sussex.
Ripples in the sand in Mount's Bay, Cornwall.

opposite, left & below right:
The beach at Horden on the Durham Coast. This piece of coastline was bought by the National Trust for £1 from British Coal in 1988 to mark the halfway mark in Enterprise Neptune's quest to acquire 1,000 miles of coast. It was an unusual acquisition as years of dumping of coal from the seams under the sea had blackened the beach, and it could by no means be described as of outstanding natural beauty. Over the course of the years, 200 million tonnes of coal had been dumped here, and in places it was 15 metres deep.

The National Trust, working with English Nature, the Countryside Commission and local authorities, instituted a millennium project, 'Turning the Tide', to create an area that is open and accessible so that people could enjoy the peace and natural beauty of the coastline. But it is the sea that has contributed to the reversing of the pollution on the beach itself, removing the spoil at a speed that has amazed. The photograph on the right shows the cleaned-up beach.

Another example of man-made pollution of the coast was the wreck of the tanker *Sea Empress* in 1998, when enormous quantities of oil were dumped on the Pembrokeshire coast in Wales. Not only was this an immediate ecological disaster, killing many seabirds such as this guillemot (opposite, above right) on a rock at Broadhaven, Stackpole, but it also had long-term implications. The oil sank to the bottom of the ocean, wreaking further damage before degrading. This killed the marine life, but in addition the Pembrokeshire coast lost a colony of bats in a sea cave, gassed by the oil when water blocked the cave's mouth.

opposite: Compton Bay, West Wight. Compton, like Alum Bay, also on the Isle of Wight, is well known for its rocks of brilliant colours, from greens through to bright orange, the result of minerals in the sediment. Whilst erosion here is of great concern, it also reveals this natural beauty. The same startling effect, with the eroded grey rock tinged with iron oxide, is achieved at Gunwalloe Bay, on the Lizard Peninsula in Cornwall.

[129]

opposite: Birling Gap in East Sussex. The sea has been eroding the chalk cliffs here for millions of years. Cottages near the cliff edge are now being threatened, and the National Trust has been under pressure to intervene and halt the erosion by building concrete walls as a defence. The Trust has opposed such measures as unrealistic and short term, arguing that the walls would only move the problem from one site to another, accelerating erosion of neighbouring coasts by interrupting the natural drift of replenishing material. This staircase at the White Cliffs of Dover (right) has been built in sections so that it can move with the cliff face.

The rising sea level is affecting all parts of the British coast. At Mullion Cove on the Lizard, Lord Robartes built a harbour in the 1890s to try to help the pilchard fishermen, following several disastrous seasons. Winter gales have battered these defences to such an extent that the National Trust had to spend £1 million in the 1990s, shoring up walls. The question is whether this is sustainable at Mullion, and indeed all around the Cornish coast – this picture shows the lighthouse on Lizard Point where the same problem prevails.

right: Dunwich in Suffolk was a major east-coast port in the Middle Ages. Now virtually all the town lies under the North Sea, and erosion continues apace. This photograph shows the clifftops at Dunwich Heath – the cliffs are receding at a rate of 1 metre each year. The National Trust has taken the decision to let the land at Mount Pleasant Farm revert to maritime heathland, thus providing a natural habitat which is now a rarity in Britain. Dartford warblers have returned, along with the antlion, which was thought to be extinct six years ago.

Coastal erosion has an impact on many of the National Trust's properties but, since it is a natural process which has formed landscapes over millions of years, it is not always appropriate for the Trust to interfere when the situation is unsustainable both economically and environmentally. The Trust's preferred policy is 'managed realignment', the idea of retreating inland, and to recommend no interference with the natural processes. At Northey Island on the upper end of the Blackwater estuary in Essex (opposite), the sea has been allowed to flood previously protected areas, again creating saltmarsh. The Trust accepts some loss or change in use of coastal land, and works with the affected local communities to alleviate the consequences.

right: A similar scheme has been undertaken at Porlock Bay in Somerset. Here the low-lying area was drained in the eighteenth century for agricultural use, but the sea wall has become increasingly difficult to maintain.

The landscape of Newtown harbour on the Isle of Wight has changed little over the centuries, and would probably still be recognisable to Sveyn the Dane, whose fleet of long-ships wintered there in 1017, the year before Canute was made king in Southampton. So important was Newtown to the defence of Southampton and Portsmouth that Elizabeth I signed a charter in 1584, entitling the borough to return two members to Parliament.

The entire Newtown estuary was purchased by public subscription in 1965 and presented to the National Trust to ensure that it was protected from the kind of development that had befallen so much of the coastline of the Isle of Wight, and of south-east England. Today it is a National Nature Reserve, an important over-wintering ground for waders and other wildfowl.

Calm and storm: Water pools on the beach at Seacombe on the Isle of Purbeck; waves crashing down on the rugged headland at Brean Down, Somerset.

next page: Whiteford Burrows, on Gower in south Wales. This peninsula of sand burrows and saltmarsh was acquired with Enterprise Neptune funds in September 1965, shortly after the launch of the appeal. In the years since, Neptune has secured over 600 miles of coastline and 52,000 hectares (130,000 acres) of coastal hinterland, and raised over £40 million.

page 144: Sunset at Woody Bay, Devon.

Photographic tours around the countryside of England, Wales and Northern Ireland,

as seen through the lenses of three leading landscape photographers:

Joe Cornish, David Noton and Paul Wakefield.

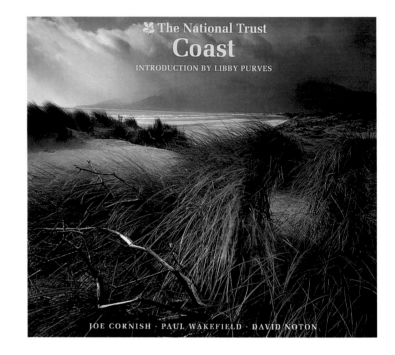

COUNTRYSIDE
With an introduction by Richard Mabey
ISBN 0 7078 0244 X
£17.99 hardback

COAST
With an introduction by Libby Purves
ISBN 0 7078 0239 3
£17.99 hardback

THE NATIONAL TRUST publishes a wide range of books that promote both its work and the great variety of properties in its care. In addition to more than 350 guidebooks on individual places to visit, there are currently over 70 other titles in print, covering subjects as diverse as gardening, costume, food history and the environment, as well as books for children. These publications are all available via our website: www.nationaltrust.org.uk and through good bookshops worldwide, as well as in National Trust shops and by mail order on 01394 389950. The Trust also has an academic publishing programme, through which books are published on more specialised subjects such as specific conservation projects and the Trust's renowned collections of art.

Details of all National Trust publications are listed in our books catalogue, available from The National Trust, 36 Queen Anne's Gate, London SW1H 9AS – please enclose a stamped, self-addressed envelope.

NEPTUNE COASTLINE CAMPAIGN

In 1965 the National Trust launched Enterprise Neptune (now renamed the Neptune Coastline Campaign) which, from the start, had two great objectives: to draw attention to the increasing pressures facing the undeveloped coast and to raise money to acquire new coastal properties and protect them for future generations. Today, thanks to the continuing generosity of countless individuals and organisations, 600 miles are safely in the National Trust's care. Most of these coastal landscapes are open to the public. They are, above all, places where people live and work, and where plants and animals can survive. Through the Neptune Coastline Campaign, the National Trust is also working to protect our coastline and estuaries and the wildlife that depends upon them.

Further information can be found on our website: www.nationaltrust.org.uk/coastline